Ruby Tuesday Readers

Stag

Beetle

By Ruth Owen

Reading Consultant:
Beth Walker Gambro

Published in 2018 by Ruby Tuesday Books Ltd.

Copyright © 2018 Ruby Tuesday Books Ltd.

Designer: Emma Randall
Production: John Lingham

Photo Credits:
Alamy: 6, 7; FLPA: Cover, 1, 20; Nature Picture Library: 8, 9, 22 (top), 23 (center); Shutterstock: 3, 4, 10, 11, 12, 14, 15, 16, 17, 18, 19, 21, 22 (center), 22 (bottom), 23 (top), 23 (bottom), 24; Warren Photographic: 5, 13.

Library of Congress Control Number: 2018906347
Print (hardback) ISBN 978-1-78856-064-1
Print (paperback) ISBN 978-1-78856-075-7
eBook ISBN 978-1-78856-065-8

Printed and published in the United States of America.

For further information including rights and permissions requests, please contact our Customer Services Department at 877-337-8577.

Contents

It is fall in the park.

A tiny animal called a **larva** is eating wood inside an old tree.

One day, the larva will become an adult stag beetle.

larva

A stag beetle is an **insect**.

The larva bites and chews wood
with its **mandibles**.

mandibles

Then it wriggles into the soil
under the tree.

The larva lives under the tree for five years.

It eats wood and gets bigger and bigger.

One day, the larva makes a **cocoon** out of soil and wood.

It covers itself in the cocoon.

cocoon

Inside its cocoon, the larva becomes a **pupa**.

pupa

Then the pupa becomes a
male stag beetle.

In spring, the stag beetle digs up to the surface.

Now he has big mandibles.

The mandibles look like a stag's antlers.

antlers

mandibles

stag

That is how stag beetles got their name.

Lots of stag beetles dig up to the surface.

male stag beetle

female stag beetle

It is time for the beetles to mate.

The male beetle flies off around the park.

wing

He looks for a spot to be his **territory**.

He will mate with the females there.

If another male comes into the stag beetle's territory, there is a fight!

They fight with their big mandibles.

They fight until one gives up and walks away.

male stag beetles fighting

The stag beetle does not need to eat.

He still has lots of fat from when he was a larva.

tongue

He licks up water with his furry tongue.

The stag beetle mates with lots of females.

three males fighting

He also has lots of fights!

A scientist holding a stag beetle.

The stag beetle lives above the
ground for about six weeks, and
then he dies!

After mating, a female stag beetle goes back to where she lived as a larva.

female beetle

She digs down into the soil.

She lays about 20 tiny eggs, and then she dies.

A tiny larva hatches from each egg.

The larvae live in the soil and eat dead wood.

larvae

In about five years, they will become adult stag beetles!

Glossary

cocoon (kuh-KOON)
A case in which some insects change from a larva into a pupa and then into an adult.

insect (IN-sekt)
A small animal with six legs and a body in three parts.

larva (LAR-vuh)
A young animal. The larvae of insects usually have long, fat bodies.

mandibles
(MAN-dih-buhlz)
The mouthparts of
some insects.

pupa (PYOO-puh)
The stage in the life
of some insects when
they change from
larvae into adults.

territory
(TER-uh-tor-ee)
The place where
an animal lives,
finds mates, or
finds its food.

Index

Read More

Ipcizade, Catherine. *Breathtaking Beetles (A+ Books)*. Mankato, MN: Capstone Press (2017).

Packard, Mary. *Goliath Beetle: One of the World's Heaviest Insects (SuperSized!)*. New York: Bearport Publishing (2007).

Learn More Online

For more information about stag beetles, go to:
www.rubytuesdaybooks.com/wildlifewatchers